This Book Belongs To

_____

Magic Moments

A BOOK OF DAYS WITH PICTURES BY

Michael Hague

Arcade Publishing • New York

LITTLE, BROWN AND COMPANY

First Edition

The illustrations for this book
are taken from the following books illustrated by Michael Hague:

Alice's Adventures in Wonderland, by Lewis Carroll
Beauty and the Beast, retold by Deborah Apy
Cinderella and Other Tales from Perrault
Michael Hague's Favorite Hans Christian Andersen Fairy Tales
Numbears, by Kathleen Hague
Peter Pan, by J.M. Barrie
The Secret Garden, by Frances Hodgson Burnett
The Velveteen Rabbit, by Margery Williams Bianco
The 1989 Velveteen Rabbit Calendar
The Wizard of Oz, by L. Frank Baum

Other images are taken from greeting cards by Michael Hague,
originally published by Oak, Ash and Thorn Ltd.

ISBN 1-55970-069-6

Published in the United States
by Arcade Publishing, Inc., New York,
a Little, Brown company

Published simultaneously in Canada
by Little, Brown & Company (Canada) Limited

PRINTED IN SINGAPORE

TWP

Designed by Marc Cheshire
1 3 5 7 9 10 8 6 4 2

MAGIC MOMENTS

1	
2	
3	
4	
5	

January

❧

Ring out, wild bells, to the wild sky,
The flying cloud, the frosty light;
The year is dying in the night;
Ring out, wild bells, and let him die.

Ring out the old, ring in the new,
Ring, happy bells, across the snow;
The year is going, let him go;
Ring out the false, ring in the true.

"Ring Out, Wild Bells"
by Alfred Tennyson

January

6

7

8

9

10

11

12

13

14

15

January

January

It was a long weary time, for the Boy was too ill to play and the little Rabbit found it rather dull with nothing to do all day long. But he snuggled down patiently, and looked forward to the time when the Boy should be well again, and they would go out in the garden amongst the flowers and the butterflies and play splendid games in the raspberry thicket like they used to. All sorts of delightful things he planned, and while the Boy lay half asleep he crept up close to the pillow and whispered them in his ear. And presently the fever turned, and the Boy got better. He was able to sit up in bed and look at picture books, while the little Rabbit cuddled close at his side.

FROM
The Velveteen Rabbit
by Margery Williams Bianco

16

17

18

19

20

January

21

22

23

24

25

26

27

28

29

30

January

January

❧

February

How do I love thee?
    Let me count the ways.
I love thee to the depth
    and breadth and height
My soul can reach. . . .

FROM
"Sonnets" by Elizabeth
Barrett Browning

3I	
I	
2	
3	
4	

February

5

6

7

8

9

10

11

12

13

14

February

15

16

17

18

19

February

At last the Prince came to a room covered with gold, and there on a bed, the curtains of which were open on either side, he saw the most lovely sight he had ever looked upon—a Princess who appeared to be about fifteen or sixteen and whose dazzling beauty shone with a radiance that scarcely seemed to belong to this world. He approached, trembling and admiring, and knelt down beside her.

At that moment, the enchantment being ended, the Princess awoke, and gazing at him for the first time with unexpected tenderness, "Is it you, Prince?" she said. "I have waited long for you to come."

FROM
The Sleeping Beauty
by Charles Perrault

February

20

21

22

23

24

25

26

27

28

29

February

❧

March

🌱

So long as Mistress Mary's mind was full of disagreeable thoughts about her dislikes and sour opinions of people and her determination not to be pleased by or interested in anything, she was a yellow-faced, sickly, bored and wretched child. Circumstances, however, were very kind to her, though she was not at all aware of it. They began to push her about for her own good. When her mind gradually filled itself with robins, and moorland cottages crowded with children, with queer crabbed old gardeners and common little Yorkshire housemaids, with springtime and with secret gardens coming alive day by day, and also with a moor boy and his "creatures," there was no room left for the disagreeable thoughts.

FROM
The Secret Garden
by Frances Hodgson Burnett

1

2

3

4

5

March

६

6
7
8
9
10

11

12

13

14

15

March

⋇

16

17

18

19

20

March

❧

The unicorn is noble;
He keeps him safe and high
Upon a narrow path and steep
Climbing to the sky;
And there no man can take him,
He scorns the hunter's dart,
And only a virgin's magic power
Shall tame his haughty heart.

FROM
a popular German ballad

March

21

22

23

24

25

26

27

28

29

30

March

March

❦

April

She was quite the loveliest fairy in the
whole world. Her dress was of pearl and
dewdrops, and there were flowers round
her neck and in her hair, and her face
was like the most perfect flower of all.
And she came close to the little Rabbit
and gathered him up in her arms and
kissed him on his velveteen nose that
was all damp from crying.

"I am the nursery magic Fairy," she
said. "I take care of all the playthings
that the children have loved. When
they are old and worn out and the
children don't need them any more,
then I come and take them away with
me and turn them into Real."

FROM
The Velveteen Rabbit
by Margery Williams Bianco

31

1

2

3

4

April

5

6

7

8

9

10

11

12

13

14

April

15

16

17

18

19

April

❧

*Thanks to the human heart
by which we live,
Thanks to its tenderness,
its joys, and fears,
To me the meanest flower
that blows can give
Thoughts that do often
lie too deep for tears.*

FROM
"Ode on the Intimations
of Immortality from Recollections
of Early Childhood"
by William Wordsworth

April

20

21

22

23

24

25

26

27

28

29

April

April

❧

May

The sun had not yet risen when she came in sight of the Prince's palace and reached the magnificent marble steps. The moon was shining bright and clear. The little mermaid drank the sharp, burning draught, and it felt as if a two-edged sword went through her tender body; she fainted, and lay as if dead.

When the sun shone over the sea she awoke, and felt a stabbing pain; but there before her stood the beautiful young Prince. He fixed his black eyes on her, so that she cast hers down and saw that her fishtail had disappeared, and that she now had the prettiest little white legs that any girl could wish for.

FROM
The Little Mermaid by Hans
Christian Andersen

30

1

2

3

4

May

5

6

7

8

9

10

11

12

13

14

May

15

16

17

18

19

May

White sheep, white sheep,
On a blue hill,
When the wind stops,
You all stand still.

When the wind blows,
You walk away slow.
White sheep, white sheep,
Where do you go?

FROM
"Clouds" Author Unknown

May

20

21

22

23

24

25

26

27

28

29

May

May

⁂

June

While yet the Morning Star
Flamed in the sky
A Unicorn went mincing by,
Whiter by far than blossom of the thorn:
His silver horn
Glittered as he danced and pranced
Silver-pale in the silver-pale morn.

The folk that saw him, ran away.
Where he went, so gay, so fleet,
Star-like lilies at his feet
Flowered all day,
Lilies, lilies in a throng,
And the wind made for him a song:

But he dared not stay
Over-long!

FROM
"The Unicorn" by Ella Young

30
31
1
2
3

June

4

5

6

7

8

9

10

11

12

13

June

14

15

16

17

18

June

A thing of beauty is a joy for ever:
Its loveliness increases; it will never
Pass into nothingness. . .

FROM
"A Thing of Beauty"
by John Keats

June

19

20

21

22

23

24
25
26
27
28

June

June

July

Cinderella found the evening passing very pleasantly and forgot her Godmother's warning, so that she heard the clock begin to strike twelve while still thinking that it was not yet eleven. She rose and fled as lightly as a fawn. The Prince followed her but could not overtake her. She dropped one of her glass slippers, which the Prince carefully picked up. Cinderella reached home almost breathless, without coach or footmen, and in her shabby clothes, with nothing remaining of her finery but one of her little slippers, the fellow of that which she had dropped.

FROM
Cinderella by Charles Perrault

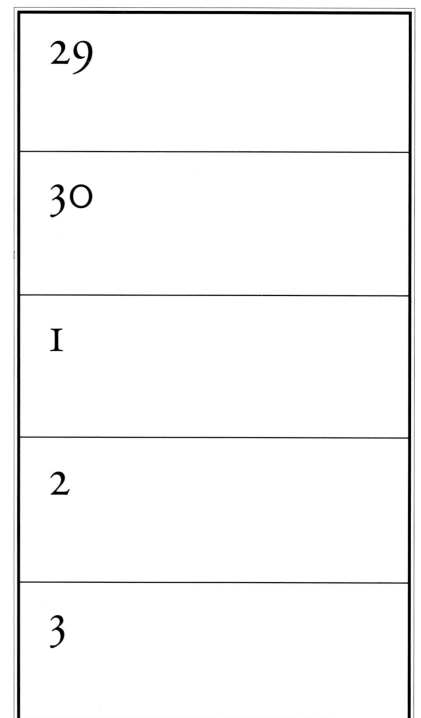

29

30

1

2

3

July

4

5

6

7

8

9

10

11

12

13

July

14

15

16

17

18

July

❧

"We must journey on until we find the road of yellow brick again," said Dorothy; "and then we can keep on to the Emerald City."

So they all started upon the journey, greatly enjoying the walk through the soft, fresh grass; and it was not long before they reached the road of yellow brick and turned again toward the Emerald City where the Great Oz dwelt.

The road was smooth and well paved now, and the country about was beautiful; so that the travelers rejoiced in leaving the forest far behind, and with it the many dangers they had met in its gloomy shades.

FROM
The Wizard of Oz
by L. Frank Baum

July

19

20

21

22

23

24

25

26

27

28

July

July

⚜

August

One, he loves; two, he loves;
Three, he loves, they say;
Four, he loves with all his heart;
Five, he casts away.
Six, he loves; seven she loves;
Eight, they both love.
Nine, he comes; ten, he tarries;
Eleven, he courts; twelve, he marries.

FROM
Mother Goose

29

30

31

1

2

August

3

4

5

6

7

8

9

10

11

12

August

13
14
15
16
17

August

❧

Alice was beginning to get very tired of sitting by her sister on the bank, and of having nothing to do; once or twice she had peeped into the book her sister was reading, but it had no pictures or conversations in it, "and what is the use of a book," thought Alice, " without pictures or conversations?"

FROM
Alice's Adventures in Wonderland
by Lewis Carroll

August

18

19

20

21

22

23

24

25

26

27

August

August

❦

September

"I felt sad at this, for it showed I was not such a good Scarecrow after all; but the old crow comforted me saying: 'If you only had brains in your head you would be as good a man as any of them, and a better man than some of them. Brains are the only things worth having in this world, no matter whether one is a crow or a man.'

"After the crows had gone I thought this over, and decided I would try hard to get some brains. By good luck, you came along and pulled me off the stake, and from what you say I am sure the Great Oz will give me brains as soon as we get to the Emerald City."

"I hope so," said Dorothy earnestly, "since you seem anxious to have them."

"Oh yes, I am anxious," returned the Scarecrow. "It is such an uncomfortable feeling to know one is a fool."

FROM
The Wizard of Oz
by L. Frank Baum

28

29

30

31

1

September

2

3

4

5

6

7

8

9

10

11

September

12
13
14
15
16

September

He did not know that when the Fairy kissed him that last time she had changed him altogether. And he might have sat there a long time, too shy to move, if just then something hadn't tickled his nose, and before he thought what he was doing he lifted his hind toe to scratch it.

And he found that he actually had hind legs! Instead of dingy velveteen he had brown fur, soft and shiny, his ears twitched by themselves, and his whiskers were so long that they brushed the grass. He gave one leap and the joy of using those hind legs was so great that he went springing about the turf on them, jumping sideways and whirling round as the others did, and he grew so excited that when at last he did stop to look for the Fairy she had gone.

He was a real Rabbit at last, at home with the other rabbits.

FROM
The Velveteen Rabbit
by Margery Williams Bianco

September

17

18

19

20

21

22

23

24

25

26

September

❧

September

æ

October

We are the music-makers,
    And we are the dreamers of dreams,
Wandering by lone sea-breakers,
    And sitting by desolate streams;
World-losers and world-forsakers,
    On whom the pale moon gleams:
Yet we are the movers and shakers
    Of the world for ever, it seems.

FROM
"Ode" by Arthur O'Shaughnessy

27

28

29

30

1

October

2

3

4

5

6

7

8

9

10

11

October

12

13

14

15

16

October

❦

"I cannot understand why you should wish to leave this beautiful country and go back to the dry, gray place you call Kansas."

"That is because you have no brains," answered the girl. "No matter how dreary and gray our homes are, we people of flesh and blood would rather live there than in any other country, be it ever so beautiful. There is no place like home."

FROM
The Wizard of Oz
by L. Frank Baum

October

17

18

19

20

21

22

23

24

25

26

October

October

❦

"You would so like to go to the ball, is not that it?"

"Yes," said Cinderella, sighing.

"Well, if you will be a good girl, I will undertake that you shall go." She took her into her room and said to her, "Go into the garden and bring me a pumpkin." Cinderella went at once, gathered the finest she could find, and brought it to her Godmother, wondering the while how a pumpkin could enable her to go to the ball. Her Godmother scooped it out and, having left nothing but the rind, struck it with her wand, and the pumpkin was immediately changed into a beautiful coach, gilt all over.

FROM
Cinderella by Charles Perrault

27

28

29

30

31

November

1
2
3
4
5

6

7

8

9

10

November

November

11

12

13

14

15

There is no frigate like a book
To take us lands away,
Nor any courser like a page
Of prancing poetry.

FROM
"There Is No Frigate Like a Book"
by Emily Dickinson

November

16

17

18

19

20

21

22

23

24

25

November

❦

The loveliest tinkle as of golden bells answered him. It is the fairy language. You ordinary children can never hear it, but if you were to hear it you would know that you had heard it once before.

"You see, Wendy, when the first baby laughed for the first time, its laugh broke into a thousand pieces, and they all went skipping about, and that was the beginning of fairies...."

"And so," he went on good-naturedly, "there ought to be one fairy for every boy and girl."

"Ought to be? Isn't there?"

"No. You see children know such a lot now, they soon don't believe in fairies, and every time a child says, 'I don't believe in fairies,' there is a fairy somewhere that falls down dead."

FROM
Peter Pan by J.M. Barrie

26

27

28

29

30

December

1

2

3

4

5

6

7

8

9

10

December

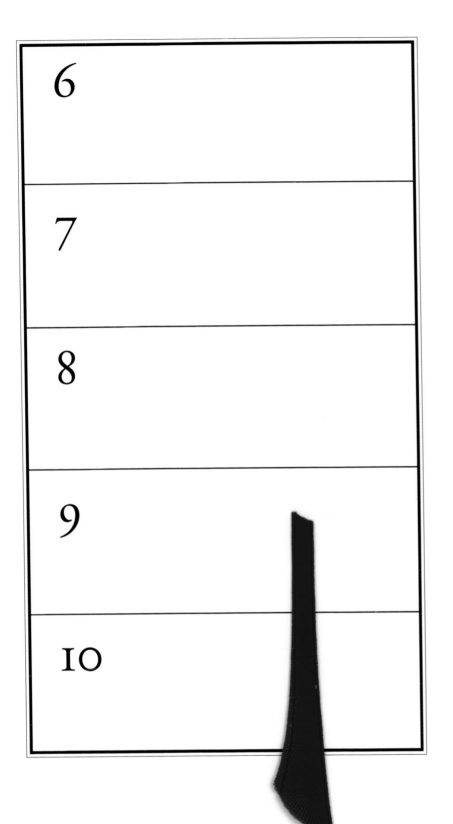

11
12
13
14
15

December

❧

The little girl lighted another match. And there she was sitting under the beautiful Christmas tree; it was much larger and more decorated than the one she had seen through the glass doors at the rich merchant's. The green boughs were lit up with thousands of candles, and gaily painted figures, like those in the shop windows, looked down on her. The little girl stretched her hands out towards them and—out went the match. The Christmas candles rose higher and higher, till they were only the stars in the sky; one of them fell, leaving a long fiery trail behind it.

FROM
The Little Match Girl by Hans
Christian Andersen

December

16

17

18

19

20

21

22

23

24

25

December

December

I heard the bells on Christmas Day
Their old, familiar carols play,
    And wild and sweet
    The words repeat
Of peace on earth, good-will to men!

FROM
"Christmas Bells" by Henry
Wadsworth Longfellow

26

27

28

29

30

December

31